CARAVAN OF THE SOUL

DEBORAH LEATHERBERY

COPYRIGHT 2019 BY DEBORAH LEATHERBERY

ISBN: 978-0-578-60770-2

BOOK COVER BYI binkski

FROM   123RF

SILLY LITTLE DREAMER GIRL

PERCHED UPON THE FENCE

OF GOD~

Contents

ANTICIPATION

Through the mist of time, we blindly go into the unknown,
Yesterday is dead and gone, buried in its historical grave.
Today is a burden, merrily we stroll along making our way.

Fighting the cobwebs stacked up against us,
A wall of stagnation that blinds us,
We attempt to make it through another day.

To be called into the arms of tomorrow.
As the loveliness of nightfall keeps us from our sleep.

Tomorrow is not promised, either is our nightly rest, lying awake,
In our beds, watching shadows that dance on the wall,
The bumps in the night send shivers through our heaps of bones.

Time is of the essence,
What an illusion,
That we have to stand here and take the blows.

What a damn shame,
That we cannot go back to where it all began,
We are life's little playthings,
Like a tetherball swinging in the unfortunate winds.

Tornadoes of situations thrown in our faces,
With the most haunting ability to numb us,
But it won't; it will keep us raw and burning.

Stopped dead in our tracks,
From achieving our lives dreams and aspirations,
At whatever the cost.

As long as we continue to play the puppet,
On the dangling swinging pendulum strings,
We have all but lost.

DIVINATION

Fear free to greet the dawn,
The expression of self-dance,
Circle the ancient ones.

The leaves dream eternal,
Echoing departure,
Waiting in the winter,
For many years.

Corpses rise out of the sea,
Trying to catch a breath.

Lost in vision,
Nearer to disgrace,
Not knowing that they are dead.

The eyes of the past blind all dreamers.

Lipstick covered youth,
Once a lonely departed young lover.

Skipping stones against the windy waves,
Of the violent seas, murky dark water.

Warmth to a touch of the cold death,
Block the bridge to the other side,
Smokey whispering demise.

Continued dreamers go on,
Against my will, late throughout the night.

Do not invite unseen guests into your home,
Pounding statues into the clay.

Let the angel of anticipation,
Drag them off into their graves.

JUST BECAUSE

Just because
People are selfish.

Just because
They cannot commit.

Has nothing to do with,
The spirit that resides in you.

It is just because
They could not handle,
The truth that you radiate.

Just because
It can cause you,
To feel less, then who you truly are.

It doesn't mean that you have to,
Let it give rise to feelings of despair.

Just because of the fact,
That you are nothing less than wonderful.

MY DEAR MOTHER

There were days,
That we went hungry but,
We never did starve,
Thanks to my mothers' undying love.

What we did have,
She would go without,
So, that we could eat.
She would just say,
"I am not that hungry!"

There were times when we were brats,
We made her scream and cuss,
But, my mother,
She sacrificed her whole life for us!

She is the greatest; A hero to us all!

Whatever I suffered,
I wouldn't change a day,
Knowing, she suffered more,
She never once did complain.

She listened to our complaints,
Had to deal with our selfish ways,
She had to worry about money,
Responsibilities and many other things.

She had to fight for her identity,
That we children tried to steal away,
She comforted us when she should have,
Thought of her own comfort, for once!

She gave and gives so freely,
Her family is all that matters to her,
She is love, and she is loved!

MY DAD

I have never seen a man,
As strong as my dad,
I have seen him come back,
From the brink of death,
Time and time again.

I hope that
I have his durability,
Or whatever it is,
That makes him tick.

Maybe it was just God,
Answering all of our prayers.

I hope that God,
Will grant me,
That kind of vitality.

What sums up my dad?

Once a Marine,
Always a Marine,
His stubborn ways,
Are part of his strength.

THE SUFFERING ROAD

I know that it is harder for those who have experienced,
Physical, spiritual, mental, and sexual abuse,
It is easy for me to sit here and say,
That the past is the past; you are going to be okay.

The only way out; that you know about,
Is to self-harm and self-medicate.

Between addiction, mental illness, and memories,
Of the horror from all you have experienced,
It makes you doubt the real you,
Whom you may or may not have ever known.

I wish that I could make it better,
I wish I had the answer,
My only advice is to take the first step,
Go out and get some help to find your way out.

Counseling, rehab,
I know it isn't cheap,
There are programs I guess,
But it is up to you to make a move.

The system has let so many down,
The stigma that haunts so many suffering souls,
Mental health resources are like revolving doors.
Government agencies couldn't care less.

I wish that I could pay the way for you,
To a new street paved with gold,
But I am not rich, and I am not God.

I AM SICK OF IT

I am getting tired,
Of hearing about people's lives,
Being ruined by alcohol and drugs.

I keep finding out,
That someone else has died.

What the hell did you do with your life?

Sometimes I can't believe it,
All you can do is pray for the addict.

It's sad and depressing,
Especially when it hits,
So close to home.

It is hard to look,
At someone you love,
Throwing away,
God's greatest gift.

The worst part is,
They don't even care or realize,
What they are doing to their kids.

The actual victims of all of this.

I don't want to call it a disease,
Maybe it is.

You eventually,
Have to take responsibility for yourself,
You need to get your priorities straight,
Before you end up in the grave.

YEARS OF TIME

These years were not wasted,
There were truth and love,
Stitched into the fabric of time.

Your vision was not blurred,
You just closed your eyes.

LOVE CHAIN

I want to teach someone,
What I can,
According to the things I know.

I don't expect you to believe,
The things I believe,
I just want to help you to grow.

There are things out there,
I cannot explain,
Still, I believe them to be true.

We reach out for the unseen,
With the faith of a child,
Trapped in the body of an adult.

We cry out in pain,
Hoping someone or thing,
Hears our cries,
Someone to comfort,
Our breaking hearts.

We go on day after day,
Trying to find the strength.

So, if I can help you,
And, you can help me,
Maybe we can,
Both help somebody else.

We are in this together,
Let's make a human love chain.

FLAWED

When life's fragrance grows pungent,
When my walk becomes redundant.

Scar tissue covered wounds,
Seep and fester,
As do the blisters on my heart.

I yearn for the burning to stop,
Pulling tight,
Around the edges of my soul.

It will scab over and fade away.

Like a grain of sand,
The dryness will one day,
Be wet with a flake of snow.

The thaw will come,
And warm my heart again,
Peace will be my spirits song.

Oh, stay calm!

When the floods flow down,
The ravine of my veins,
Bringing me back to life again.

NATURE, MY ANCESTRAL SONG

Words are written,
With each drop of rain,
Songs from the sparrow,
Spring forth in protection.

Wind in the wild grass,
Orchestrates each tune,
Snowy, bough branches,
Creaking in rhythm.

Melody, of the flowing stream,
Echoing throughout the prairie,
Where my ancestors rest.

Across the raging sea, they came,
To America's shore of independence,
Freedom to each new generation,
To think and say what needs to be heard.

FIREFLY

Fireflies dream brightly,
Glowing in abandon shine.

Fluorescent in the meadow lonely,
Lighting up the sky.

Dawn comes,
Spirits are breaking.

Until again,
The yonder night.

SILLY LITTLE DREAMER GIRL

It's inevitable; you said, looking down heavy-hearted,
The tears don't matter anymore,
Stuck inside your own crazy head,
You cannot escape it; you cannot erase it,
You created it; Now, you embrace it.

It is a dream in your heart, an illusion that blinds your eyes,
From the realistic nature,
Delusional grandeur dancing with your mind,
Yet, you continue to believe all its' lies.

You are a hopeful waif, a silly little dreamer girl,
It is not likely to ever open up and be on your side.

Still, you think that you deserve something,
Like courage, faith, and the hope of deliverance,
From the hell that you have created for yourself,
A hand out of the quicksand that is filling up your lungs.

The princess (or Is it a prisoner?)
In the high castle tower of your own making,
Tumbling, as the earthquake razed it all down to the ground,
Walls of terra-cotta crumble around you.

You cry tears of ash and soot,
You taste the dust in your mouth.

DEPRESSION

This is just a stagnation depression,
You can't do anything about it,
You just sit there; you have lost all hope.

It is the same thing day after day,
You have to find a way to change.

Get up and do something,
Get out of your comfort zone.

Find a hobby,
Go somewhere outside of your front door,
Find a new hero that is not on TV or computer.

Get yourself together; life is too short.

I know you think it is easier for me,
To say this to you, then to do,
I speak from experience,
I have been there too.

Everyone feels that they are right,
About their own way.

You believe this; I believe that,
Someone else believes differently.

The funny thing is,
We are all wrong.

Life is a fragile gift bestowed upon ignorant souls.

BUILDING BLOCKS

Give your children,
Some building blocks,
Spoil them if you want,
But, give them,
Something to build on.

Don't leave them,
Out in the elements,
Blinded by the snow.

Don't make them,
Spend their whole life,
Wondering which way,
They should go.

Unfeeling and yet,
Feeling unloved!

Even if you don't know,
What you are doing,
Or how to do it.

Fake it until they make it and,
Hope that they get through it!

GRATEFUL

My cup of blessings,
Runneth over.

My cup of vision,
And, anticipation,
Lie empty,
Of accomplishment.

I am very grateful,
For what I have.

I am hungry,
And longing,
For what I want.

Don't play,
With broken glass,
You will cut yourself,
My dear one.

SUBMERGION

How dark is your heart?
How morose are your thoughts?

You stand at the edge of the sea,
You are afraid to jump in,
Because you know that,
It is sink or swim.

You, my friend, are afraid to drown.

No one ever taught you,
Any survival skills,
You don't have a life raft,
So, you can't hold on.

You feel yourself go under,
The weight of life's water.

You bob up and down,
And hold your breath,
As you float into a dreamlike state.

No one tried to save you,
Until it was way too late.

DIVINE

Do you really expect me to believe that,
A human father of the Prodigal,
Is it more capable of compassion than our loving God?

A God who tells us that we,
Must love our neighbors as ourselves.

And, while the whole world,
Slaps us in the face,
That we must turn the other cheek.

But, that a God of mercy,
Is it not willing to give us the same courtesy?

Because there is not one adequate father,
On the face of this earth, who would send the child,
That he professes to love to an eternal hell.

The fact that he is a Holy God,
Already proves that he is better than us,
Mere Human beings,
Who are incapable of loving as he loves.

Yet, here we are,
Unless we are full of abusive behavior,
Giving our children all of the support we can,
So, that they can turn out to be decent humans.

I am not trying to be a false prophet but,
I guess I need to learn Hebrew, Aramaic, and Greek.

To read it as it was written,
Because It is my belief,
That his words got lost in translation.

ROBBED OF EVERYTHING

I was not able to sit Shiva,
When my parents died,
How could I?

They were gassed,
In the shower of a Polish town.

They, along with,
Most of my family were burned in the ovens.

I only hope that the murderers,
Choked on the ashes of my people!

I was not able to place a pebble,
On the headstone of my loved ones.

They are gathered in a pit,
Where abouts are unknown.

I escaped,
How? I don't know.

Left to live,
The rest of my life, trying to forget.

RUIN

Before all of the drugs and the drama,
Back when you
Still loved your daddy and your momma.

When you still had a sense of purpose,
Before you started doing all of those things,
That hurts us.

We hate to see you go,
Through all of these trials,
What can we do,
When a kid goes buck ass wild?

You might be of legal age,
But you are still our child.

There is nothing we can do about it,
Except to hope and to pray,
That we never see them in ruin.

How do you stay mad,
At someone you love?

Even when they are over there,
Taking all of those drugs,
Wreaking havoc on the whole family.

Your mad at the fact that they are dying,
Over something stupid like getting high,
Yet you feel guilty for being mad or hurt,
Because you love them at the same time.

HYPOCHONDRIAC

Why would you will yourself weak,
To the point of making yourself sick?

I can't figure out if you really believe it,
Of if you are only trying to gain attention.

I know you don't want to go to work,
Who does?

That is not a reason,
To will yourself bedbound.

I know that there are invisible diseases,
I don't think that is the case with you,
You lied about having cancer.

Was all the pity worth it,
Until everyone found you out?

No one believes anything you say,
You are a pitiful disaster.

When you cannot gain attention,
For your ailments,
You then, turn all Munchausen by proxy,
You project fake illnesses upon your children.

You obviously are mentally ill,
So maybe you do deserve pity.

I, for one, would just rather,
Stay far away from you and your drama.

A TRACE OF MYSTERY

Someday God might ask me,
"Do you want me to give you
Something to cry about"?
You have had it way too easy,
For way too long,
All you do is walk around,
Faithless, in doubt.

You are like a little nymph,
Sleeping on a sunflower.

At night, the fireflies,
Beam all around you,
You cannot see that,
They are your guiding light.

You would rather,
Live in a dream,
Then to open up your eyes.

Suddenly, when things fall apart,
You always seem so surprised.

You have this one-possession,
A gift that you cannot keep,
Still, you chase it down,
Because you are a big girl now.

Scoop up the gold stars,
In the reflection of the sea.

Let it drip,
From the palm of your hands,
Leaving a trace of mystery.

HYPOCRITE

Who brutalized me,
With all of these lies?

I thought I knew,
What the truth was,
Until I was told otherwise.

I was raised to believe,
My parents' mores,
Without a chance,
To think for myself.

I want the right,
To believe what I want,
Without being made to feel,
Like I am guilty of a crime.

If I am not hurting you,
Or anyone else,
Then it should not matter to you,
What I do with my life.

It is hard for you to realize,
That you do everything,
That you want to do,
The very same things as me.

It is different,
When you can't view it,
With your own set of eyes.

You can't have,
The same perspective,
When your mind is totally blind.

PSYCHOPATH

You are pouring it on a little thick,
Acting like a crazy bitch.

I think that they need to up your meds!

You don't have a filter anymore,
Do you even hear yourself?

I think it's a Freudian slip,
You didn't mean to say it,
Yet, you meant every word,
That proceeded from your lips.

You don't even care,
What people think but,
We all know that you,
Are nowhere close to innocent.

Stop trying to play the victim,
You brought this shit upon yourself.

You are crazy as hell,
Although you play normal pretty well,
For those who don't see the real you.

NOTE TO MANIC SELF

Love died brighter,
Then the noonday sun.

When and why did I,
Stop doing cartwheels,
When will I start again?

A dying lady bit me,
A shade of yellow,
You have never seen.

Unless death is wearing,
Its' favorite color,
Our breath,
Is the pulse of the earth.

I want pennies from heaven,
I think that I deserve it.

Haters who tried to trip me up,
Who tried to cause me self-doubt,
Don't worry about it; I worked it out.

For the love of God,
Shut your stupid mouth,
You never stop; it is all nonsense.

I know you want to feel important,
Yes, your opinion matters,
As much anyone else.

You run on manic energy,
You have nothing to say,
You only want to hear your own voice.
.

JUNKIE

You never thought it would go this far,
You never thought it would last this long,
Now, you find that you are barely holding on.

You say it doesn't matter,
It can't change you,
You have your habits; you say that you can quit,
When you don't,you feel like a fool,
You start treating everyone like shit.

So, what are you going to do?

You say love can't give you what the needle can,
Your nerves are fragile, and you want to be alone.

You hope to get it straight,
But you can't handle your pain,
You want to go back in the past,
You know that you just can't.

You are too blinded to see any future,
Until you can't stop.

You won't try, and you can't cry,
Because you are so hollow inside.

We reach out to you with love,
But a feeling blinds you,
You are too numb,
To respond to our hearts.

We cry and pray for you,
We want you to be clean again,
Please try to reach deep down inside,
And pull yourself out of this hole that you are in.

FAÇADE

She ran off to Hollywood,
To chase all of her dreams,
Only to find herself living on the streets.

California is the place to go.

You can find a job,
For minimum wage,
Yet, still not make the rent.

Dare I,
Mention starvation?

But at least,
She stayed thin.

COMES BACK ON YOU

Everything you do,
Comes back on you,
Suddenly the abuser,
Becomes the abused.

When one's power is gone,
But the others have not,
That is when,
All of the hatred comes out.
Should we feel sorry,
Or, just sit back and,
Watch the show,
Let us see how far it will go.

When the former has gone,
It will be the newest ones turn,
Someday, they will grow old,
The circle rolls on and on.

HIDEAWAY

I was trying to make a favorable argument,
I am awake, but my vision is a little blurred.

I was talking to my husband,
And five of his cousins.

You are not competing,
As bad, as those, on the street corner,
Where relationships break down.

I see the hallows of my face,
As I linger slowly.

I want to capture the moon and,
Put it aside for a rainy day.

Whenever I am feeling down,
I will make it my hideaway.

BLESS US

Leaves tumble down gently,
From trees that fall hard.

A manifestation of hopes, dreams,
And nightmares.

They are identical,
Except they are reversed.

Your brain stops,
Feeding your body and,
It is only 5 P.M.

Life can be so hard,
Even though we are so blessed,
We stress about this world.

See, to me,
I am not the odd one out,
Everyone else is.

Your childhood lies,
In a vast sea of emptiness.

You had to grow up hard,
You had to grow up fast,
I wish that I could bring you back,
From the dead but, I just can't.

We don't know what can happen,
From one minute to the next.

We have to stay humble and pray,
God continues to bless us.

THE STORM

The night wears on,
From across the room.

The proceeding storm lies ahead,
The hearths' shine reflects the fires' glow.

We can read by the firelight,
The stove can keep us warm.

Snowblind by the light of day,
We have 24 hours to go.

The cyclone bomb is on its way,
To burst forth in radiance,
And to bury us in snow.

THE STORY OF LIFE

All we can do is live our lives,
In this space and time that we are given.

We may never know who we have touched,
Or the joys we have sown, if any.

Always hoping and praying,
That things will turn out for the best,
Or as they should, according to Gods, will for us.

We don't be kind,
Because we want to be repaid tenfold,
But deep down in our hearts,
We really hope we will be.

The waters flow day by day,
Down the waterfall of good cheer,
Let the smiles that we bring reflect our own,
Each and every year.

We cry our tears,
Because we are human,
And, life is hard,
There is so much suffering in the world.

We wish upon a falling star,
To leave nor feel any scars,
Hoping others' tears were not our cause.

Humbly plodding on and on,
With the faith that God,
Will bring us safely through,
To the other side.

SNAP OUT OF IT

You walk through the cool breeze,
In the middle of the night.

Will you make it back home safely?

Will you be alone all of your life?

You seem like a child,
Running, from what you know,
Crying for what will never be.

The children you long for,
Because you think that,
They will save you and make a man stay.

If you had that,
Would you still be hollow inside?

Because of that dream,
You forget to enjoy your life,
You forgot about all of the things that you have.

Because in your eyes,
None of that can save you.

You think your salvation comes,
In the form of a baby or even worse, a man.

I DON'T NEED YOU

You came along, just like a song,
You turned my whole life upside down.
What do you think I feel for you now?

I gave you my love,
I did everything I could.

I thought we'd be friends,
Until we were dead,
Now I don't know,
Where this thing ends or begins.

I think my life,
Is better off without you,
You are so full of pretense.

WINTERTIME

A snowflake landed in my eye,

And, absconded away with my sight,

When it suddenly disappeared,

My vision was so much clearer,

Without blur nor stagnation.

LADY LIBERTY

The stars shine down,
Through the night time sky.

Softly, landing in the harbor,
Floating gently to the shore,
Shining their light,
On the tiptoes of liberty.

She is the lady who makes,
A million dreams come true.

Let us bask in her freedom,
The lady that we love.

BURIAL GROUND

Everything,
You have shown me,
Has been apart of my life.

I am satisfied,
To dance through this place,
As long as I hear your voice.

I know who I am,
I know what I am.

I don't know,
Where I am going but,
I know where I have been.

I feel like I have been,
In a burial ground all afternoon.

I feel like,
You can lift me up,
If you wanted to.

THE WINDS EMBRACE

The wind caresses me,
In the most unusual way,
It blows my hair around my face.

In the lonely mist,
I try to find my way.

It is hard to believe,
In something that I cannot see.

It is hard to trust when I,
Do not know what to expect.

It is hard not to flinch,
Once experiencing neglect.

What we believe,
What we teach ourselves to see,
What we allow ourselves to feel,
It is all a dream.

THE FROST

Crisp,
Ice-covered flowers,
Eventually,
The thaw comes to melt.

Unlike,
The crystalized hardness,
Of my heart which,
My soul cannot dissolve.

The freeze,
Is stronger than the heat but,
Not so much as against the burn.

CLOUD OF HOPE

Notwithstanding,
The miserable situation,
I guess conditioning,
Can be achieved.

If I close my eyes,
And grasp at straws,
Trusting all of my schemes.

I turn away to hide my tears,
While standing strong,
To face my fears.

I pray that this is not what,
My life will always be,
I hope to live and grow.

I hope to attain,
What I can't let go of,
Even if I cannot see,
The joy or misery it will bring.

I hope to be free.

Before I know it,
It will be time for me to leave.

I hope that the part of me,
Which spends most of the time in a dream,
Will continue to do so until it comes true.

TOO FAR FROM YOURSELF

Even after tomorrow comes,
I know you won't be so far away.

Even when you try to run,
You go from day to day.

You will be alone,
No matter who you are with,
Until you learn how to self-love,
The character that; is you.

You need to realize,
You cannot run away,
Not from me or anyone else.

I have learned to believe that,
You can never escape yourself.

THE MOON IN JUNE

The soft clouds swiftly drift,
Over the light of Luna,
The crisp cold air kisses my skin,
Even though it is nearly June.

I gaze up at the stars,
That chase the sun,
As I find the luckiest one,
I blow a kiss,
Up to the man in the moon.

Looking down from the sky,
He sees me gazing,
From the window of my room.

Searching for his face,
My eyes are fixed,
Upon the moon in June.

MY LITTLE COUNTRY HOME

Look at the flowers blooming,
Behind the garden gate,
So beautiful and strange.

The grass needs to be mowed,
It is all patched with brown.

It is good to be out of the city,
Where the tall buildings,
Shade the warmth.

A cold hatred floats,
Over the atmosphere,
Every night and day.

The street musicians,
Make it worth the while,
For a short visit but,
Not an extended stay.

I love to hear them sing and play,
Until the sky pours down,
Chasing them all away.

I am glad to get out of the city,
For the weekend,
With a return to my abode,
In my little country home.

KNOWLEDGE

Even when I swear, I am right,

I am more than likely wrong.

When I think that I am wrong,

I am probably wrong.

Which makes me right,

At least half of the time.

VEILED

Dark are the secrets,
That are kept hidden from sight.

Jewish, Nazi Germany,
Whose children have to hide.

Learning the catechism,
In catholic orphanages,
In order to stay alive.

INTENT

She forges on,
Through the dark night, the wind,
The rain and the snow in her face,
Up the mountainside, she goes.

She turns around,
She looks down, the village lights,
Sparkle like diamonds in the night,
Through the misty clouds.

She cries,
For what she has to let go of,
As icicles form on her cheeks.

She gathers her composure,
She walks on not knowing,
Where she is going or,
Where she will end up.

What will she find?

What can she keep?

She is out there searching for love,
Not realizing that she had it all along.

Yet, it is a journey she must go on,
In order to see the truth for lies,
To see the forest for the trees.

Her family and loved ones pray,
Let her find her way back home someday.

Help her to find what she is looking for,
In her travels of life, please, keep her safe.

ASPIRATIONS

If all I get is one,
Then one is all I got,
I have to take a deep breath,
To find the faith and strength,
I need to take that shot.

I want to say something meaningful,
To someone who is hurting and needs to hear it.

I want to hold the hand of a child
Whose life has just begun,
I want to comfort the dying.

I have to get my mind,
In the proper perspective,
Otherwise, I cannot be objective,
That is no good for anyone.

I need to get out of my own head,
I need to think about someone else for a change.

But will I?

I am very selfish,
That is where the trouble lies.

I have big dreams and high hopes,
Will, I crash and burn,
Will I soar high into the sky?

I have not achieved any,
Inclinations,ambitions or expectations,
That I have put into my mind as of yet.

I have not disregarded my dreams,
I will not capitulate, and I will not forget.

COVENANT

Sitting in the dark,
Bargaining with the Lord.

Making promises,
I have no intention of keeping.

If I am being honest,
I am hoping he doesn't know this.

Of course, he does!

Maybe my heart he will not see,
Perhaps he'll let me go on dreaming.

Will he forgive me?

Of course, he will,
For God is love,
That is what he does!

DIGNITY

You cannot fall in love every time,
Someone smacks you on the ass and calls you pretty.

You need to take an in-depth look,
Within your soul,
You need to find some self-esteem.

You shouldn't fall in love,
With every stupid fool that comes around,
Right after being dumped by another.

You should find someone,
Who loves you for you.

You need to find someone,
Who lives to fulfill all of your wishes,
Because that is what real men do.

LIFE IS SHORT

Don't be a fool,
Get your ass back in school,
Before you get too old,
Or forget what you know.

Because time flies,
Life is short,
Before you know it,
It is all gone.

I know that you think,
That you have time,
So, did I.

You don't want to spend,
Your entire adult life at a menial job,
Get a career that will enable you to retire,
With benefits and a 401 K.

One that will carry you,
Throughout your whole life long.

DEPARTED

We are cursed,
To carry blessed memories,
The burden and yearning,
Crying out for our dead.

Not hearing their voices,
Hugging their bodies,
Kissing their lips,
Nor seeing their faces.

Void of comprehension,
Of their wisdom and advice.

The memories become affliction,
With the knowledge,
That they are gone,
Forever, from this earth.

Unbearable, to our broken hearts,
It is so hard to breathe, sometimes.

RUNAWAY

I don't want you to be around,
To see me fall,
Knees first on the ground.

You will never understand,
Why I have to let go of your hand,
I don't understand it myself.

It is not pleasant, but I have to run away,
Nothing is right, so I turn a deaf ear,
I cannot accept you or anyone else's advice.

This is my song to sing,
I have to do it in my own tune,
Unfortunately,
That note does not include you.

I push you away,
Because I cannot commit,
It is the fear in me,
That keeps me from you.

I wish that I could keep you near,
But that is not fair to you,
So, I hope you will just forget me,
Because I cannot stay with you.

PAIN

I couldn't find my dreams,
Because I was so busy,
Listening to my fears.

Falling apart at the seams,
And drowning in my own tears.

I never thought that soon,
A new day would come,
To save me from my pain.

Got to the point to where,
I didn't even care anyway.

Yet, I continued to make it,
Through each and every day.

TIME REWRITTEN

We have all undergone,
A technological transformation,
That has catapulted us,
Somewhere that we would,
Rather not have been.

Then there is life in general,
That keeps moving us along.

We make our way,
Down the road less traveled,
In the dark, with our nap sack,
Full of faith, hitched upon our backs.

We have no choice,
But to go down the path before us.

There is no turning back,
We have come too far,
If we are lucky, we can sojourn.

Keep your eyes ahead of you,
As you wander down this trail,
Keep on going, don't look back.

Yet keep the memories,
Deep inside your soul,
They are the truths of life,
Whether they are seen or not.

They are souvenirs,
You cannot let go of,
The love that will always remain,
Deep inside of our hearts,
Spirits, souls, and minds.

GRIM REAPER

He rises from the murky bog,
With a scythe in his hand.

His black robe dangles,
On his bones.

They call him the reaper man.

He desires to ruin happy people,
He comes to collect the sad.

There is no escape.

Sooner or later,
We are all at his command.

MY DEAR FRIEND

When I was a child,
I made a wish; I had a dream.

I counted on this wish to come true,
More than I counted on reality.

I waited a long while,
Am I waiting still ?
Through frustration and despair.

I lost my hope,
I lost my dream,
I lost everything.

You have given this all back to me,
You make me confront myself,
By helping me see,
I am as good as anyone else.

Something I never did believe before.

All I know is that you are a good friend,
The only one who ever understood,
The things that I stand for.

You get me.

Now, very much unlike a child,
You have given me the strength and,
The encouragement to face my life.

You have given me a world,
That I can now grow old in.

ACCEPTANCE

Maybe you didn't waste,
My precious time,
Being with you, after all.

Maybe I wasted my time,
By staying with you,
For way too long.

Who knows,
Maybe, I wasted,
Your precious time,
Then again,
You did lead me on.

You could have told me to go.

Maybe we both thought,
That there was something there,
Perhaps we were both wrong.

Imagining each one,
Or the other could be,
The only true one.

Maybe we were,
Just holding on,
Until someone,
Better came along.

OUT OF THE OLD COMES THE NEW

The fear of being washed off the rocks,
By the raging sea,
Does not make you weak.

Going under the spell of all, your lost dreams,
Drowning in the swirling and treacherous waves.

That is what scares you!

What is, what was or what could be,
Reaching out to you,
Because you reach out to me.

You understand and lend a hand,
That pulls me up out of the water and,
Onto the tranquil sand of sanity.

Maybe what should have been,
Still, can someday be.

A rebirth of all of those,
Lost dreams of you and me.

MEMORIES

As I sat here thinking about all the things,
That I have done in my life,
I can't help laughing about all the times,
That I thought of my blessings as strife.

I laugh at the feelings that I had.

At the stupid things I did,
To make myself feel better.
.
It is so unimportant now.

In years to come, I will remember,
The things that thrill me now.

Reflections in the back of my mind,
About how dumb it all seemed at that time.
.
Now, is what I believe in!

Just like fashion,
It too, will all fade away and,
Be my memories of yesterday.

BIPOLAR

I don't medicate,
I ride through the pain.

Sorry for the inconvenience,
To everyone around me,
Who has to feel the repercussions,
Of my independence from substance.

No, I don't medicate,
I embrace the pain.

I will be in control,
Of what I say and do.

If I am going to be a fool,
I cannot blame it,
On pills, drugs, or alcohol.

BLIND

If I could see my life through your eyes,
Or, even so through the eyes of a child.

Maybe things,
Could seem clearer to me,
I could see who I really am.

Notice changes in myself,
That has to take place.

If I saw myself,
Through someone else's eyes,
I could learn to understand my own thoughts,
Maybe, I could love myself instead of despise.

I could see that I am not as bad,
As I have always thought myself to be.

Maybe I would see,
That there are some people,
Out there who, sometimes,
Might even look up to me.

DREAMS

I've made a lot of foolish choices,
Listening to the voices in my head.

Letting them guide me,
To places, I never should have been.

Telling me lies,
Like love never ends,
And dreams never die.

I have seen them,
Fadeaway and disappear,
As fast as day turns into the night.

Never to be seen again.
These dreams, I dare not dream.

I have seen all of the danger,
And escaped it,
Until the day I met you.

DISASTER

You are a disaster,
Just look at yourself.

Think about what you have become.

I hope you realize someday,
That you are living your life all wrong.

I hoped that you would hurry up,
I wish that you would come back home.

Please don't be forever gone.

FORMALITIES

Why go through the formalities,
Just to make everything look legit?

You already know,
What you are going to do,
You are so full of shit.

Why do you tell,
All of your stupid lies,
Time and time again?

You should just give up and quit,
Because you are never going to win.

You think that you know it all but,
I have seen the color of death.

Let me tell you now,
It is something you don't soon forget.

It looks just like the sound of,
Someone gulping for their last breath,
The eyes that go lifeless,
Losing color, just like the flesh.

So, don't give me your formalities,
Because just like the families who cry,
History has a way of eluding us with time.

FRIEND AND STRANGER

You are an old friend,
Turned stranger.

I still remember who you are.

I love the things we did,
Oh, what danger.

I cherish,
The words you said.

I know,
You did not lie to me.

We have kind of lost touch but,
Deep down in our hearts,
We both know that we will never part.

When life begins,
To become too much,
Just know,
You have my love.

EMPOWER YOURSELF

You have to empower yourself,
That is another song I sing to myself.

Do something,
You have never done before,
Nor never believed you could do.

Rejoice,
In the success or failure or,
Even for the attempt.

Read a book, a hard read,
Hell, write a book,
Even if it's an easy read,
Nonsense or make-believe.

Maybe no one wants to read it,

Don't get depressed,
If it doesn't come out,
The way that you hoped it would.

At least you did it.

Yes, my friend,
Empower yourself.

STARDUST

Stardust falls,
From the heavens above,
Trying to enchant my soul.

I will not be a fool for,
The moon and the stars,
With all of the false dreams,
That they hold.

I fight the mirages,
Dancing in my head.

I will not lose myself,
Or my mind to a whim,
A calling from the stars,
The moon and the sky.

It is not reality,
It is just a lie.

DON'T GIVE UP

You have waited long enough,
Your proverbial prince will never come.

Sometimes it is hard,
Sometimes It kills deep down inside.

You tend to depend on others,
I know what that feels like,
I am guilty; I have done it also.

You go do what you have to do.

You have to find yourself,
Don't let the pain or fear stop you.

Pick up your butterfly net,
Run through the grass so green,
Capturing all of your crazy dreams.

Hold on for dear life,
They are all you have.

You enkindle gifts and talent,
It is there,
I know it is because I have seen it.

Stop waiting,
For someone to do it for you,
Go take a walk,
On the cloud with the silver lining.

Go to attain all that you are willing to work for.
.
Cross your fingers,
Say a prayer,
If anyone deserves it, you do.

CHANCES

I make new observations every day,
Shaking my head in total disbelief,
It won't ever go away,
Because it is a new world that we live in.

I am going to take every chance I am given,
We all think we still have time,
So, we procrastinate until the day we die,
Leaving our dreams in the wake of life.

HELL

I can't get up,
So, I will go down deeper,
To the pit of hell, if I have to.

It is not a choice,
Just a chance.

To see if I can,
Crawl up and out.

With my fingers bleeding,
My flesh hanging,
All around my jagged nails.

You need to realize,
That I will punish myself,
To, in turn, punish you.

You don't know how far,
I am willing to go.

You don't know,
What I will do,
In order to protect,
My loved ones from you.

SURVIVAL

There is a lot to say,
About getting gone,
There is so much more,
To talk about when you get home.

You can float,
On the life raft of survival,
You can drown,
In the deep, dirty water of the sea.

You can either sit on your couch,
You can go out into the world,
To make a name for yourself.

You can fall down,
On your bended knees and pray.

You can hope
You can wish,
You can imagine,
Day after miserable day.

Sooner or later, you will find,
Until you do something,
It is never going to change.

MOURN

Unkept, unclean, and unshaven,
Dangling my cold bare feet.

I look to the mirror but,
The thick, dark cloth erases,
The sadden reflection from my sight.

It seems like yesterday,
We engraved your name on the headstone.

With tears filling our eyes,
We gathered to intercede for the dead,
To recite the mourner's prayer.

It's been 30 days,
My beard hides my face,
My hair is long, and so out of place.

We are so heartbroken,
That our lives will never be the same.

KARMA

The evil you project,
Makes you so smug,
With your black heart and words.

It will catch up to you,
And when it does,
I am going to sit back and laugh.

It is going to bite you in the ass,
And when it does,
I am going to watch it with joy.

I will pray that God will give you,
A taste of your own medicine.

I don't like to be so vengeful,
But you have gone overboard.

It is not going to be me who stops you,
Call it what you will.

Karma,
You reap what you sow,
What comes around goes around.

Whatever it is,
It is going to knock your ass on the ground,
I can almost taste it in my mouth.

Enjoy your little, happy power trip,
Soon, Karma will make you it's bitch.

LIFE'S MOUNTAIN ROAD

Life's' road is covered with snow,
Please, walk-in my footsteps,
If they help you to stand and grow.

If one footstep of mine,
Should cause you to fall,
Then child, do not follow me at all.

As we climb life's mountain,
I will pull you up along the way,
By my side is where you belong,
Each and every day.

If I get weak and lose my grip,
Forgive me, child, if I make you slip.

Hold strong, when I am not,
Pull me up with your smile,
It means the whole world,
Because you are my heart.

God, give us a brand-new day,
So, we can start all over again.

Let us please you,
Where we failed yesterday,
Please make it better again.

DON'T PITY ME

"Do you only like dead flowers?" she asked me,
Her voice deep in concern with despair for my soul.

"You sit in the dark all alone," she adds,
"What a sad life you must have."

I tried to explain that I was okay,
I wanted to reassure her that I liked it this way.

Her face so full of pity,
As she looked down on me,
I just smiled back up at her,
As the light reflected tears in her eyes.

.

DEMAND SOME RESPECT

Why would you allow someone to beat on you?
Degrade you or stalk you like an animal?

You are worth more than you think,
You can do better, and you deserve better.

Have some respect for yourself,
I am telling you it is better to be alone,
If you can't find someone else worth your while.

I am telling you to demand some respect for yourself.

What will it take until you love yourself?

The antagonist will not change for you,
No matter what you do,
Because he is a narcissist.
The drugs and alcohol fuel his fire,
He is not worth any amount of your desire.

Get rid of him,
Demand some respect for yourself.

TROUBLE WITH WOMEN

Girls like to be smothered,
In what they perceive to be as love,
They want to sit there,
Hug, hold their man's hand,
Kiss, get flowers and a ring.

That is their way of feeling loved and validated.

Men don't feel that way; men want to be left alone,
They want sex, but they want to be free.

They don't want the responsibility,
Of making a woman feel whole,
The more you treat them like shit,
The more they like it and respect it.

That seems to be,
What makes a man want to be with you.

Because you are living your life,
Blowing their minds,
Not expecting you, to expect him,
To make your life complete.

The more you show them,
That you are strong on your own,
The better you will get along,
When women are too needy, men run away to escape.

Be strong, self-validating, independent and whole,
Without relying on a man to give you these things,
Because he can't, He won't.

Go out and be yourself,
No more pretending…No more being clingy,
Believe me, girl,
You are going to be fine on your own.

YEARNING YOUTH

I have let life,
Get the best of me,
I forgot how to laugh,
I forgot how to dream.

I am trying hard,
To take charge and change,
I dig deep down inside myself,
To find out who I truly am.

They say you are nobody,
Until somebody loves you,
It has always been that way for me.

I am beginning to realize,
I have to believe only in myself.

I have waited so long,
For someone to save me,
From my lonely pain.

I have wasted many years,
Waiting for someone,
To rescue me from me.

STOP ACTING STUPID

We all want attention,

To be validated,

We want to receive accolades.

Maybe that is what I am trying to do,

By writing this book,

But this social media has become too much.

Pretending to be happy and normal,

From what I can see, they are not.

I have seen young girls with their boobs in their hands,

I guess trying to impress some man or someone,

I have seen way too old of folk trying to act young.

Not by using filters on their pictures,

We all, in vanity, do that.

It may feel good to have an audience,

But we are not 19 anymore,

We all need to grow up and stop acting stupid.

MEMORIES

I remember when we met,
A long, long time ago,
In a place so different,
From the world we had known before.

I remember the time,
I first looked into your eyes,
I remember hoping someday,
I could make you all mine.

I remember our friendship,
It's so hard to believe,
It disappeared in a vapor-like dream.

I think of a time when,
We would laugh and sing,
Of course, beforehand,
We indulged in a drink.

I remember a time,
When you were mine for a while.

Somehow, we let it all go,
So, I will remember you with a smile.

TRUST ISSUES

I trusted you, unknowing,
Undauntingly, I believed in you,
Isn't funny how fast we let things roll?

How far, into oblivion, it all went,
Now, I am left here standing,
Alone in the dark.

The stupidest things about women are,
We want someone to love us,
To make our lives fulfilled,
We think we can trust men,
What fools we become in the end.

That is our own fault, we believe,
In fairytales with happy endings,
Because that is what we were taught.

I wanted you to want me,
The way I wanted you,
I was too needy,
I realize now that chases people away.

After the "newness" wears off,
Things die down and fade away,
You pledged your undying love to me,
You assured me that was not the case.

I felt happy and secure for a little while,
I was on cloud nine; after I fell hard for you,
You went and changed your mind.

Even before I met you,
Because you are, after all, a man,
I knew it, subconsciously,
Deep down inside,
You were nothing but a liar.

THANK YOU, GOD

Considering the circumstances,
Of this current situation,
That I have no say in.

Others may look to enchantment,
Or transcendence, I turn to prayer.

I am not in control of anything,
But I know the one who is,
He has never let me down, as of yet,
I don't expect that he ever will.

He got us through another New Year,
Some of us, by the skin of our teeth,
But here we are…

Thank you, God!

TENDER KISS

It's a lonely life just sitting around,
Waiting for love to knock on your door.

If you open it when it is not time,
You are going to get hurt for sure.

If you wait too long,
It is going to pass you by,
You will never know,
What you have missed.

Love is a little bit more,
Then one heated moment,
In the tenderness of a kiss.

EMBRACE THE PAIN

What we have,
It is just no damn good.

All the things,
That we said we'd do,
Deep inside my heart,
I knew that we never would.

Time has a way,
Of getting in the way,
Hope has a way,
Of getting misplaced.

Time does not change anything.

It only makes us use to it,
It allows us or causes us,
To embrace all of the pain.

I AM

I am,
All of the things my eyes have seen,
All of the places that I have been.

I am,
Made up of hopes and dreams,
Irish blood; and, Celtic beams.

I am,
Part of a family tree,
Whose genetics are out of control,
It is hard to put the brakes on hold.

We do what we want, not what we are told.

Because of the things that I have learned,
Because of all of the lessons in this life,
I am, who I am, take me or leave me,
As I shift the gear into overdrive.

ALCOHOLIC

You are always sorry,
You are always ashamed,
But yet, you never change,
It is always the same ol' thing again.

I realize you are crying out for help,
But no one can help you,
This is a battle you have to fight yourself,
You cannot see that it is your decision alone.

Do you love your family,
More than you love the bottle?
Because you are losing everyone.

No one wants to be around you,
It is never any fun when you are drunk.

You are emotionally, mentally,
And, sometimes physically,
But mostly spiritually exhausting.

You say you only throw out hurtful words,
Because you are backed up into a corner but,
You are the one who created the corner.

In fact, there is no corner,
Until you, in your drunken stupor,
Start all of your drama.

Bringing everyone down with you,
Because misery loves company,
Maybe you will change someday,
But I don't see it.

It is devastating,
When you lose hope,
For the recovery of someone you love.

K.S.U

The lines were drawn, and sides were taken,
In a crowd, some children played,
The men in their mask shot off their tear gas,
We will never forget the price that was paid.

They tried to say that no one gave the order to shoot,
Yet, bullets filled the air,
A volley of shots rang out, reaching every ear.

You were innocent, but the people found you guilty,
Your sentence was death,
You walked across the campus,
The soldiers turned; their bullets pointed you out.

There were so many there that day,
Somehow, the conclusion only reached four.

As you lay murdered,
The American people yelled,
"There should have been more."

Brothers and sisters mourn for you,
Mothers and fathers could not understand,
It has been many years,
Your ideas, never to be fulfilled.

Our numbness reminds us that,
Our American dream of peace and love,
In reality, it is one nation under violence and fear.

Now we see daffodils,
Instead of blood,
Flowing on this ground.

Flowers are better than bullets,
We remember the war in Vietnam,
We think about the day America killed its own.

DEATH

Sooner or later,
Death knocks at our door,
A time will come,
When we cannot cheat death anymore.

Sometimes we see it coming,
We welcome it with open arms,
Because our loved one,
Has suffered so very long.

Sometimes, unknowingly,
Selfishly we want them to stay,
Even when we know that they,
Are in so much unbearable pain.

Regardless of the time,
That we think we have,
Life will fade away.

We will be together again,
Some glorious, golden eternal day.

I AM A FOOL, BUT HE IS NOT

Praise the king of everything,
God's love is sent down and raised again.

Crushed and bruised,
Pierced hands and feet.

He took my blame,
What sacrifice.

HE IS

He is,
My refuge.

My calm,
In the midst of the storm.

He is,
My salvation.

He is,
Almighty God.

He is,
My protection, my redeemer.

He is,
My salvation, my creator.

FAITH

Life is so much better,
When you let go and let God.

Stop obsessing over things,
You cannot control.

Stop trying to save souls,
That are not yours to save,
You are only chasing people away.

Trust is the keyword,
Don't stop believing,
Continue to pray and have faith.

YESTERDAY

If my life was over tomorrow,
What would you do?

Please do not curse the Lord,
For taking me from you.

God gave us one another,
To keep each other strong,
You know, that one at a time,
He will call each one of us home.

Praise the Lord and thank him,
That he felt we were unique enough,
That he gave us one another to love.

Live your life for God,
We will be together again.

What we shared on earth,
Will surround us once more,
Only this time, it will never end.

If your life is over tomorrow,
I will remember the fun we had.

The things that we said,
That we would do,
But never found the time,
I will do in memory of you.

Take the time out to say,
The things that you always wanted to say.

It may be too late tomorrow,
To wish for yesterday.

MORE BOOKS BY THIS AUTHOR

MUSINGS, DREAMS, AND OTHER SILLY THINGS

FROM THE MIND

OF AN UNCOMMON WOMAN

www.ingramcontent.com/pod-product-compliance
Lightning Source LLC
Chambersburg PA
CBHW031538040426
42445CB00010B/595